EMPATH

*How to Create Your Shield Body
That Will Protect You Forever*

by

MIKE LEE

INTRODUCTION

I want to thank you and congratulate you for downloading the book, *"Empath: How to Create Your Shield Body that will protect you forever"*.

This book has lots of actionable information on how, as an empath, you can create a shield body that will protect you forever.

Do you feel overwhelmed whenever you are in crowded and noisy places? Do you feel frustrated when you hear other people's worries and concerns? Do you often think about the worries of others more than you do your needs? Do you remain depressed and stressed whenever you meet negatively charged people? Can you easily sense the feelings and moods of complete strangers even before they tell you something?

If you can relate to any of these instances and these occurrences happen often, it is very likely that you are a gifted person: an empath, a person with a special ability to understand and perceive the feelings, emotions, and thoughts of others. More than that, you also possess the power to absorb those feelings and perceive them as your own.

When you are constantly soaking up a plethora of emotions, you spin out of equilibrium and become confused about your own emotions, needs, and feelings. This confusion can often lead to a state where you ignore your needs and wants and instead worry about the needs and wants of those around you, the very issue that chains you to stress, anxiety, and depression.

To overcome these problems and to make good use of your empathic abilities, you need to gain better insight into your ability and learn how to create a shield body that protects you from an onslaught of emotions and stress. Your shield body is an armor of energy that protects you from the negativity around you. Your shield body keeps you from behaving like an emotional sponge.

If you would like to know more about your empath abilities as well as how to create a shield body, this book will help you with that. Designed as the ultimate empath's blueprint, this book has every piece of information on what empaths are and can do, along with actionable information on how to protect your energy from the negativity around you, and how to use your ability to build an empowered life.

Start reading this guide NOW! It will guide you and help you forsake a negative life in favor of a positive one.

Thanks again for downloading this book. I hope you enjoy it!

© Copyright 2017 by Mike Lee - All rights reserved.

This document is geared towards providing exact and reliable information in regards to the topic and issue covered. The publication is sold with the idea that the publisher is not required to render accounting, officially permitted, or otherwise, qualified services. If advice is necessary, legal or professional, a practiced individual in the profession should be ordered.

- From a Declaration of Principles which was accepted and approved equally by a Committee of the American Bar Association and a Committee of Publishers and Associations.

In no way is it legal to reproduce, duplicate, or transmit any part of this document in either electronic means or in printed format. Recording of this publication is strictly prohibited and any storage of this document is not allowed unless with written permission from the publisher. All rights reserved.

The information provided herein is stated to be truthful and consistent, in that any liability, in terms of inattention or otherwise, by any usage or abuse of any policies, processes, or directions contained within is the solitary and utter responsibility of the recipient reader. Under no circumstances will any legal responsibility or blame be held against the publisher for any reparation, damages, or monetary loss due to the information herein, either directly or indirectly.

Respective authors own all copyrights not held by the publisher.

EMPATH

The information herein is offered for informational purposes solely, and is universal as so. The presentation of the information is without contract or any type of guarantee assurance.

The trademarks that are used are without any consent, and the publication of the trademark is without permission or backing by the trademark owner. All trademarks and brands within this book are for clarifying purposes only and are the owned by the owners themselves, not affiliated with this document.

TABLE OF CONTENTS

Introduction 2

Understanding Empaths and Their Special Gift 7
    Signs and Symptoms of Being an Empath 8

Types of Empaths 12

How to Protect Your Energy by Creating a Shield Body 16
    What a Shield Body Can Do for You 17
    How to Create Your Shield Body 18

Clearing Energy Blockages by Balancing Your Chakras 27
    Understanding the Role of Chakras in Balancing and Growing Your Energy 28
    7 Chakras in Your Body 30
    How to Restore Balance in the 7 Chakras 33

Using the Power of Meditation to Protect Your Energy Shield . 42
    A Quick Insight into Meditation 42
    How to Practice Meditation 44

Additional Effective Energy Shielding Strategies 48

Conclusion 52

Before we can get to a point of learning how to build the shield body that helps you to reduce the extent to which you absorb the emotions of others, it is important that we build an understanding of what being an empath truly means. Let's begin.

UNDERSTANDING EMPATHS AND THEIR SPECIAL GIFT

An anonymous empath once uttered the following truer than true words:

"An empath truly feels what the other person is feeling. If someone is constantly negative, bitter, or upset all the time, I end up feeling negative, bitter, and upset all the time. If someone is happy and cheerful all the time, I feel happy and cheerful too. I absorb the emotions of those I interact with. It can be wonderful, but it can also be very exhausting. And it can be incredibly confusing to determine which feelings are my own and which are someone else's."

The feelings of this anonymous empath aptly describe what being an empath feels like. So who exactly is an empath? Well, an empath is someone who has a heightened power to sense emotions, feelings, and moods. If you are upset and there is an empath around you, that empath will know that you are not feeling alright the minute he/she sees you or interacts with you even if you do not willingly share anything with him/her. Therefore, if you have the ability to sense what someone is feeling, if you feel presences around you, or can sense the type of aura a person has, it is very likely that you are an empath.

To determine if you truly are one, here are a few signs and symptoms that will reveal if you indeed are one.

Signs and Symptoms of Being an Empath

If you know you are an empath, great; at least you know why you feel exhausted and drained all the time and know where your energy goes even when you have not done anything fatiguing.

On the other hand, if you are still unsure about why you have a heightened sense of sensitivity, or why you vividly feel the emotions of those around you, here are some signs and symptoms you should look for in yourself to understand if you are an empath.

1: You are Super-Sensitive

Perhaps people have told it to you a hundred times and even though you keep telling everyone you are not sensitive, the truth is you are.

If you feel the happiness and sadness of those around you 100 times more than they do, if you cannot stop thinking of someone's misery or joy, if you feel mentally and emotionally disturbed upon seeing a disturbing photograph or hearing bad news, if you are hyper sensitive to loud sounds and crowds, and cannot bear small injuries and pains, you are a gifted empath.

Since empaths have a highly sensitive brain, they feel everything more than other people do. That is because in an empath, the part of the brain associated with feelings and empathy are more active than in other people. This also proves that being an empath is an inborn ability: it is something inbuilt in you—something you cannot change or nurture. You are either an empath or you are not: there is no in-between.

2: You are an Emotional Sponge

Not only do you feel the emotions of those around you, like a sponge that soaks up as much water as it can when placed in a bowl of water, you also absorb all those emotions. If whenever you interact with someone, you end up feeling overwhelmed with emotions, both negative and positive or one of the two, that is because you are an empath, and as such, absorb other people's emotions very fast.

3: You are Compassionate and a Good Listener

Because of your heightened sensitivity, you nurture a lot of compassion for those around you and are always ready to lend a keen ear to anyone who wants to pour out his/her heart out to you. Not only that, you also love helping those in need and try your best to be there for everyone and anyone who needs your help and sometimes even those who do not want your help.

4: You are incredibly Imaginative

Empaths' heightened sensitivity opens up their imagination, which gives them the ability to perceive different things differently. If you are extremely imaginative and enjoy creativity, thank your empathic gift.

5: You Do Not Know How to Differentiate Your Emotions from Those of Others

While being compassionate is a big plus to being an empath, this gift also brings with it a lot of confusion and pain. Empaths often lack the ability to distinguish between their emotions, needs, and feelings from those of others.

If you treat the pain of others as yours and often brim with emotions even when nothing tragic or pleasant has happened to you, it is mainly because you do not know how to discern between your feelings and those of others.

6: You are highly intuitive

Since an empath can easily feel the presence of things around him/her, he or she is quite intuitive and knows when something is about to happen. If you have a super-active intuition and always seem to know when something has happened or may happen, it is because of your empath.

7: You Feel Presences around You

If you often feel a presence around you even when you cannot see someone, or if you often invisible forces around you, you are likely to be an empath. Some empaths have the ability to feel spirits and receive messages from the spiritual world. We will talk more about this in the 'type of empath' section.

8: You Frequently Experience Chronic Stress and Physical Issues

Because empaths feel everything, sometimes 100 times more, they experience quick emotionally exhaustion that causes chronic stress and other health problems. If you constantly complain of feeling stressed even when you have not done anything taxing, and if you experience constant digestive issues, backaches, and headaches, pile blame on your empathic ability.

Being an empath is an amazing thing since this ability helps you gain insight into what people think, feel, want and how they behave. In addition, your heightened sense of compassion makes you a favorite in your social circles. However, like everything else, this gift comes with a cost too: the cost of feeling emotionally swamped and emotionally drained.

This mainly happens because you do not know how to use your gift properly and effectively or how to keep yourself from emotional drains. Do not worry; this book shall teach you a fantastic and effective way to protect your energy and cleanse yourself of all the negative energies. Before we move to that, we first need to understand the different types of empaths so you know the type of empath you are.

TYPES OF EMPATHS

Most empaths are in the habit of wearing someone else's shoes and feeling things as that person does. The common belief is that empaths can only sense the feelings of humans around them. However, this is not true because some empaths have the power to receive signals from most things around them; from physical objects, to plants, to animals, to invisible forces, empaths can feel them all.

In this section, we shall discuss the major types of empaths; this will help you identify the type of empath you are:

1: Emotional Empaths

Emotional empaths are the most common empaths. If you are an emotional empath, you pick up the feelings and emotions of those around you and perceive those emotions as yours. This is exactly why you experience a saturation of dissimilar emotions and feel confused about your feelings.

2: Medium Empath

Medium empaths are empaths with an ability to feel, hear, and even see spirits, usually of deceased individuals. If you often feel different presences around you, and have encountered unexplainable situations that seem the doings of invisible forces, you may be a medium empath.

3: Medical/Physical Empaths

Medical empaths feel the energy emitted by the bodies of people around them. If you can feel the energy emitted by a person's body, and can feel when someone is feeling sick, you are likely to be a medical empath.

For instance, if you met someone whom you felt was going to become very sick soon and soon after, your premonitions came true, that is because of your ability to pick up energy from people's bodies.

4: Animal/Fauna Empaths

Fauna empaths have a strong bond with animals. They feel strongly connected to animals and can feel their pain, joy, and other emotions. If you have a natural likeness for animals, cannot bear seeing them in pain, always rush to help abandoned or ailing animals you see on the road, and seem to know how an animal feels, you are an animal empath.

5: Plant/Flora Empaths

Like animal empaths, plant empaths can feel the needs, wants, and emotions of plants. They know how plants feel and are aware of their needs. They have a knack for growing beautiful plants. If you seem to know your way around any garden, feel alive when you are around plants and greenery, and can sense the mood of the plants around you, you are a flora empath.

6: Claircognizant Empaths

Claircognizant or intuitive empaths know when something is about to happen or when someone is about to do or say something. If you always seem to know when someone is telling lies, know when someone is scheming against you or anyone else, and know when something is about to happen, you are likely to be an intuitive empath.

7: Psychometric Empaths

These empaths can receive signals, energy, and information from material objects such as furniture pieces, books, photographs, gemstones, jewelry pieces, etc. If you can feel the vibrations of different inanimate objects, absorb their energies, and receive signals from things around you, you are a Psychometric empath.

8: Place Empaths

Place empaths are empaths who feel drawn to certain locations or places, and extremely drained in others. If you have always imagined yourself living in a certain place, feel drawn to a particular country or location, and get good vibes when visiting certain places, that is because you absorb energy emitted from places and locations and are a place empath.

9: Geomantic Empaths

Geomantic empaths have the gift to feel the energy and signals from the Earth and soil. If you correctly predict the occurrences of natural disasters such as earthquakes and hurricanes and can pick up signals from the ground by touching it, you are a geomantic empath.

Observe your feelings, emotions, and behavior for two weeks and see how you feel around different things, people, places, plants, and animals. By doing this, you will figure out the type of empath you are.

Once you have decoded that mystery, it is time to move on to the next phase: cleansing yourself of unwanted energies and learning how to protect your energy from constant interruptions and depletions.

The following section discusses this aspect.

HOW TO PROTECT YOUR ENERGY BY CREATING A SHIELD BODY

How does being someone who is constantly picking up new emotions from every angle feel? Well, it as simple as "annoying and frustrating". You have a gift that needs proper usage and channeling so you can use your sensitivity, creativity, and intuition to build a beautiful and meaningful life for yourself and others.

Because of your inability to discern between what is and is not yours, and your ability to behave like a radio that picks up different radio signals, you cannot focus on your needs and well-being.

To avoid negativity, stay calm and stress-free, and build a positive, worthwhile life, you have to learn how to cleanse your body of all the negative, extra, and undesirable energies you habitually pick up. While you do that, you must also learn how to protect your energy from sabotage or depletion so it stays intact and can help you live a better life. This is where building a shield body comes in.

What a Shield Body Can Do for You

Your shield body is a shield of energy you visualize around your body that acts as a protective armor that protects you from infectious undesirable energies. Your shield body is an armor that keeps negative and any extra energy from entering your body and messing up with your energy, emotions, thoughts, and feelings. With your shield body around you, you start feeling safe, happy, and calm.

This shield of energy protects your inner energy from other poisonous energies, which in turn gives your internal energy a chance to flourish. When no extra energy enters your body, you start to focus more on yourself and gain a better understanding of your needs, wants, emotions, feelings, desires, and thoughts. This helps you distinguish your emotions from those of others.

Moreover, you gain better control of your energy and can regulate it. Before building your shield body, you do not have control over how and when your inner energy moves out of your body, which is why you feel fatigued all the time. However, when you learn to draw your shield body, you gain control over how your energy moves and if you want, can send it out to anyone and at any time. As an empath, you can only find solace when you protect your energy and keep it intact; by creating a shield body, you can easily achieve this.

Let us discuss how you can create a shield body:

How to Create Your Shield Body

The process of creating your shield body has five steps/phases. Different experts describe the process differently, but the steps and results are more or less the same. Below is a systematic guide you can use to build your shield body and use it to clear your body and mind of undesirable emotions and protect your energy from negative energies and emotions.

Step 1: Tune into Your Emotions and Feelings

To practice the process, find a quiet, peaceful, safe, and clutter-free place, corner, or room. If the room is messy, untidy, or full of distractions, clean and clear it of all the unwanted things and make it clean and tidy. Why is this important? Well, because it becomes easier to focus on the practice when you are in a clean and peaceful environment.

Ensure the area you choose is perfectly safe for you. If you feel unsafe in that environment, change the location and find a safer one. Doing this is important because that is how you will learn to pay attention to yourself and respond to your needs.

Once you find the right environment, sit in a chair/sofa, on a yoga mat, or lie down on your bed, floor, or the yoga mat in any way you like. Close your eyes and take slow, calming, and deep breaths. If your normal breath lasts 3 or 4 seconds, prolong it to 5 or 6 seconds. Inhale very deeply to a count of 5 or more, hold that breathe to another count of 5 or more, and then exhale deeply and slowly to a final count of 5 or more. Breathe in this manner for 5 minutes or for as long as it takes to feel calm.

When you feel about 60% calmer than before, gradually shift your attention to your feelings and emotions. Let your mind loose and focus on the different emotions you feel. If you find yourself feeling angry, concentrate on that emotion and explore it deeply. Ask yourself questions such as:

"Why do I feel angry?"

"Do I feel angry because of something I did or something that happened to me or has this anger rubbed on me from someone else?"

"How do I really feel?" Ask yourself other such questions.

This practice helps you take inventory of your emotions and thoughts, which allows you to understand your emotions.

When you dig deeper into how you feel, you start to understand that most of what you feel does not really belong to you: someone has bestowed it upon you, unwillingly. This realization helps you distinguish your emotions from those of others, which helps you stop picking up the sentiments of those around you. Keep exploring different emotions for as long as you like and once you gain command over discerning between what is yours and what is not, move to the next step.

Step 2: Clearing Unwanted Energies and Emotions

When you are in a better emotional state, have a clear view of your emotions, and know how to distinguish them from those of others, start clearing yourself of all the extra energies, emotions, and needs that clog up your energy. At this point, you are just aware of the emotions that are not yours but to purge of all the stress they bring you, you need to clear those emotions and unwanted energies.

To do that, visualize yourself standing underneath a beautiful waterfall made up of bright, glowing light. Visualize the light flowing from the waterfall and falling all over you, covering every inch of your body. As the light covers your physical body, it starts penetrating your external body to enter your mental and emotional body too.

The light has a special power: it has the ability to wash away all the tensions, worries, concerns, emotions, thoughts, feelings, wants, and energies that do not belong to you and are not yours to bother with.

As the light enters your body and soaks up your emotional body, it washes away all the emotions, needs, feelings, and energies you earlier identified as someone else's. As the light dismisses all the energies and sentiments that are not yours, you feel lighter, fresher, and calmer than ever.

Take as much time as you need to visualize that light washing away all the unwanted and extra emotions and energies. When you feel your body now only has the thoughts, feelings, sentiments, and energies that are yours, imagine the light slowly moving out of your body and into the soil. As it gets into soil, the soil absorbs it and it disappears.

Although the white light has left your body, it has left behind its remnants. Since it has cleared your body of all undesirable and extra energies and sentiments, it has cleansed you and given you a beautiful glow. That glow is your energy: it is yours to care for and maintain. This energy is what you need to protect yourself from sabotage by outside elements and to do that, you have to grow it. The next step allows you to achieve this goal.

Step 3: Filling Your Heart Center with Pink Light

Your body is glowing with a beautiful white light emanating from within. To make this energy bigger, better, and stronger, slowly bring all your attention to your heart center: the center of the chest.

Visualize a gorgeous fountain of a soft pink light radiating from the center of your heart and slowly filling your body. As you visualize, take slow and deep breaths and imagine the pink light growing bigger and stronger with each breath.

Visualize the pink light quickly reaching every part, corner, and organ of your body and filling it completely. As you visualize this scenario, you will actually start feeling stronger and more peaceful within. Since pink is the color of calmness, visualize a pink color filling your body and consequently soothing you.

When the pink light has enriched your entire body, visualize it flowing outside of it and covering a distance of around 3 feet around you to form a gorgeous aura of pink colored light. Savor the amazing new aura you have created: this aura of energy protects you from everything you do not want to enter your body and mind and meddle with your peacefulness. This is your loving space that will protect you from all sorts of negativity and to ensure it does the job well, you have to protect this energy. The next step tells you how to do that.

Step 4: Protecting Your Energy Space

To protect the beautiful energy you just created, imagine a huge, strong, and amazing shield of bright, golden light emerging just outside your glowing pink bubble of energy and slowly covering the entire bubble. The golden shield completely surrounds the pink bubble and has no weak point or opening that can allow unwanted elements entry into your pink bubble. As you visualize this scenario, keep breathing deeply.

As you imagine the golden shell surrounding your bubble of energy, repeat positive suggestions/affirmation that make you feel that nothing wrong can happen to you as long as you remain protected by your energy bubble and the golden shield around it.

Affirming positive suggestions means you will have to say positive things that make you feel strong and positive. When you repeatedly say something to yourself, you affirm it to your subconscious. When your subconscious accepts a suggestion, it produces similar thoughts that make you believe in the suggestion and that attract similar experiences towards you.

When you affirm things like "This energy is mine and it helps me stay positive and strong," or "I am the owner of my energy and everything in my body and mind happens as I want," you actually start to believe in these suggestions. When you staunchly believe in something, you start behaving accordingly too.

When you affirm that without your permission, unwanted elements cannot gain entry into your body, mind, and energy space you created, you will start being more aware of the different stimuli around you and will pay close attention to the different sentiments and information you receive from those around you.

If you feel a certain emotion can disturb you, you will instantly stop focusing on it and because you will not focus on it, it will not disturb your energy. This awareness helps you separate your emotions from those of others and keep the latter from disturbing the beautiful peace and energy you have built inside and around you.

After shielding your energy bubble, move to the next step that helps you take a final inventory of your emotions and thus better understand yourself.

Step 5: Reflect on Your Emotional State

Now that you have cleared yourself of negative, debilitating, and unwanted energies and emotions, and have built, as well as protected your energy bubble, take a final inventory of your emotions so you can figure out if the stress you felt earlier has vanished or not.

Tune in to your emotional state again by taking long, deep, and cleansing breaths. Bring your awareness to your sentiments and focus on any sort of pain, discomfort, or stress you feel. If you do not feel any sort of discomfort, stress, anxiety, or negativity, it is clear that the discomfort you felt earlier was courtesy of the sentiments you picked up from someone. Since you have cleared these unwanted elements, the related stress has vanished too leaving you calm and peaceful.

However, if any sort of stress or negativity still remains within your body and mind making you feel stressed, the feeling belongs to you. You need to explore and investigate the feeling some more to know why it is pestering you. If you feel anger bubbling inside you and it has not cleared away even after practicing the cleansing process, it means the anger is yours.

Investigate that anger by asking questions such as:

"Why do I feel angry?"

"Am I angry because someone said something hurtful to me or because I am disappointed in myself?"

"For how long have I been feeling this way?"

"When was the last time I felt this angry?" Ask yourself other similar questions that help you deeply analyze that emotions and understand its root cause.

Ponder upon that emotion for as long as you deem fit and avoid labeling it negative, bad, or unhealthy. By labeling emotions as negative or bad, you associate them with negative sentiments that continue upsetting you long after. Therefore, make sure you do not do that.

If you do not feel like focusing on a certain emotion that has been upsetting you for a long time and exploring it brings back upsetting memories, end the session instantly and appreciate yourself for being so strong. You can try again the next day or whenever you feel comfortable. To continue working on assuaging all your worries as soon as possible and keep growing your energy, it is best that you stay regular with the practice.

Your energy grows stronger and flows freely throughout your body when there is no sort of negativity blocking it. Since stressful or painful emotions bring stress into your body, it is best to get rid of them on time so they do not debilitate your energy or decrease it.

Now that you know how to cleanse yourself of all sorts of unwanted and negative energies, emotions and sentiments that upset and divert your attention from your well-being, habitually practice this process every day.

Start by doing it every day in the morning and as you go to bed. Doing it in the morning refreshes and energizes you, giving you the energy to stay strong the entire day. Doing it before you sleep helps cleanse off negativity or extra energy you have picked up during the day so you clear it before resting.

To build the habit of doing this every day, set compelling rewards you can enjoy when you practice the process every day in the morning and at night. For instance, if you are a chocolate aficionado, treat yourself to your favorite chocolate whenever you practice the process twice daily for 5 days. Rewards stimulate you to stick to good behaviors and make them a constant in your life.

Once you can easily practice the process twice a day, try doing it each time you enter a social situation, move to a crowded place, enter a new venue, prepare to meet a stranger, after traveling and whenever you feel overwhelmed. All these situations have the potential to overwhelm and upset you and can infect your energy bubble. Clearing and protecting your energy before encountering these situations keeps you peaceful and happy.

While this process certainly does wonders for your energy and helps you safeguard it, you also need to clear energy blockages because doing so ensures your energy bubble stays sound and strong. In the next section, we shall discuss how to do that.

CLEARING ENERGY BLOCKAGES BY BALANCING YOUR CHAKRAS

Many healing and spiritual disciplines believe that every living and non-living thing in the world functions because of its innate energy. All living things get their energy from the cosmic energy flowing in the universe.

Similarly, we function because of the flow of energy in our bodies. When the energy flows smoothly, we function well, experience no mental or physical issues, and feel good about ourselves.

However, when we feel some sort of pain, problem, or health condition, it is mainly because of an energy blockage in one or more energy centers in our body. The energy centers in your body are called chakras and to protect your newfound inner energy from any unwanted external force, you need to stabilize your chakras.

Let us find out what chakras are, the chakras in our body, and how balancing your chakras can help unleash your true potential as an empath.

Understanding the Role of Chakras in Balancing and Growing Your Energy

Chakra is a Sanskrit word that means wheel and since the chakra in your body spins energy, we can call chakra the wheel of energy. There are more than 114 chakras in your body but the 114 are the prominent ones. These chakras are the junctions at which energy stops for a while and then moves forward. These chakras are triangular but since they are always spinning energy and moving at a high pace, we call them energy circles or wheels.

Of these 114 energy triangles or chakras, 2 are outside your physical body and of the 112 located inside your body, you can work on only 108 since there lacks proper documented text of the location of the remaining 4 and because these 4 usually flow as a result of the energy flow in the 108 chakras.

Of these 108 chakras, only 7 are of utmost importance. These 7 chakras (in this section, we shall discuss the location and description of each) regulate the energy flow in the other 101 chakras and your entire body, which is why these 7 chakras are the most studied and discussed.

The 7 main chakras are responsible of regulating energy throughout your body and mind. When the energy in your body flows smoothly and without interruption, you feel at peace, and when you are at peace, you can easily focus on yourself, your needs, and your energy.

When there is smooth energy flow in your body, you feel calm and peaceful and can think clearly. This improves your sense of awareness allowing you to distinguish between your feelings and those of the people around you. This keeps you from absorbing any extra emotions, which allows you to concentrate on your well-being. Naturally, when you focus on yourself, your energy thrives.

As opposed to this, when an energy blockage occurs in any of the 7 chakras, you experience physical, emotional, mental, and spiritual relative to the blocked chakra. For instance, if there is blockage of the chakra regulating your health, you will experience a health related problem. Naturally, when energy does not flow easily and freely throughout your body, you feel ill at ease, something that affects your pink fountain of energy and the golden shield that safeguards it.

When you feel disturbed and stressed, focus on cleansing and protecting your energy becomes harder, which weakens the golden shield resulting in leaks and openings. This exposes the shield to undesirable external forces and elements that soon break past the shield, gaining entry into your energy.

When undesirable outside elements such as unhealthy emotions, thoughts and sentiments, infects your pink energy, it starts to weaken. Obviously, when the protective energy inside you weakens, you easily succumb to overwhelming emotions, thoughts, and the needs of others, and start focusing on them once again.

As an empath, you are bound to be compassionate towards others, which is amazing but a constant flood of unnecessary thoughts and sentiments keeps you from finding the purpose of your empathic ability and keeps you from unleashing your full potential. To ensure that does not happen to you and that you keep enhancing your energy so you can use its full power, balancing your chakras is paramount. To achieve this goal, let us discuss the 7 chakras in your body and how you can balance the energy flow in them.

7 Chakras in Your Body

Here are the seven chakras:

1: Root Chakra

This is the most basic of the 7 chakras; it is positioned at the root of your spine, right in your tailbone. It is in charge of keeping you grounded and regulates your emotional issues as well as your financial independence, monetary issues, and issues related to food.

When energy smoothly flows in this chakra, you feel happy with yourself, feel grounded and humble, experience no monetary or financial issues, and have no food related problems too. However, when the energy in this chakra is out of balance, you experience all types of issues in these areas.

2: Sacral Chakra

Representing your connection to new people and experiences, as well as your ability to accept new people and scenarios, this chakra is located about 2 inches beneath your navel in your lower abdomen. It is in charge of your sexuality, pleasure and pain, emotional and physical well-being, and sense of abundance. When there is an energy blockage in this chakra, you go through problems in the aforementioned areas.

3: Solar Plexus Chakra

This chakra is in charge of your sense of self-esteem, self-image, and self-confidence; it is located in your upper abdomen. Your self-image is how you perceive and view yourself; your self-esteem refers to how much or how less you value yourself, and your self-confidence refers to your faith and belief in yourself and your abilities. When there is an energy blockage in your solar plexus chakra, your self-esteem, self-image, and self-confidence start to dwindle and you feel unconfident of yourself.

4: Heart Chakra

Governing your ability to give and receive love, the heart chakra is just above your heart in the middle of your chest. It governs emotional areas related to inner peace, serenity, joy, and love. An energy blockage in your heart chakra makes you feel frustrated, depressed, and agitated.

5: Throat Chakra

Located in your throat, this chakra governs your ability to express your feelings, speak and manifest the truth, and communicate well with those around you. When an energy imbalance occurs in the throat chakra, being honest becomes difficult, you experience problems expressing your feelings to others as well as communicating your needs to them, and have trouble easily interacting with others.

6: Third Eye/Brow Chakra

Representing your ability to concentrate on your goals and the bigger picture in life, this chakra regulates your imagination, intelligence, intuition, wisdom, and decision-making abilities. It is located right on your forehead between your two eyes. When an energy blockage occurs in this chakra, you find it harder to connect to your intuition, experience trouble being imaginative, and find it difficult to make important decisions.

7: Crown Chakra

Of the 7 and the other chakras in your body, this is the highest; it signifies your connection to your spiritual side. Located on the top of your head, this chakra governs your spirituality, and your perception of beauty and bliss. When there is an energy blockage in this chakra, you cannot tap into your spiritual side and your perception of beauty becomes distorted too.

Balancing these 7 chakras in important to all of us, but doing so is more important to empaths. Since empaths feel everything multiplied a gazillion times, as an empath, you are likely to become more sensitive to the different issues you experience because of energy imbalances in any chakra.

To keep your energy intact and strong, and to make it flow smoothly throughout your body, balancing the chakras is imperative.

Here is how you can do that.

How to Restore Balance in the 7 Chakras

Meditation and visualization are arguably the two best ways to cleanse your chakras of negative energies and energy blockages and to restore balance in them. We shall discuss meditation separately (in the next section) since it is a big subject that has many benefits.

Here, we will focus on visualization and how it helps restore energy balance in the 7 chakras.

Visualization is the use of imagery to imagine things as you want to be. When you imagine good things happening to you and think of having achieved your goals, you program your subconscious to think positively or as you want. This improves your frame of mind, and helps you think positively and believe in yourself. When you visualize clearing your chakras of all energy blockages, you eventually start believing in their cleansing, which actually leads to that very thing.

Each of the 7 chakras in your body has a specific color depending on the type of vibration of the chakra and the frequency that radiates through the chakra. White light consists of seven colors and when light enters your body, it becomes disintegrated into its 7 color components.

1 of the 7 chakras absorbs each of the 7 colors depending on the frequency of the colored light and the vibration of the chakra. To use visualization to cleanse your chakras, you have to imagine the corresponding light of the chakra filling it up and cleansing it. Let us see how you can complete this process with each of your 7 chakras.

The image below shows the colors of the 7 chakras: each color of the chakra is located in the chakra's position.

Root Chakra

The color of the root chakra is red which symbolizes survival, safety, groundedness, and staying nourished. To cleanse your root chakra, sit peacefully and comfortably in a quiet spot, preferably with your eyes closed. Take a few deep, cleansing breaths like the ones you took when cleansing and protecting your energy.

Next, think of the position of the root chakra and then imagine a bright, red colored light entering your body from the Earth and filling your spine. Imagine this light cleansing your root chakra of any sort of negativity and your root chakra spinning fast and smoothly without any interruption.

Think of your root chakra sprouting roots that slowly extend towards your lower body and move out of it. As the roots move out of your body, they start to penetrate the Earth grounding you to the soil. Practice this exercise for 15 to 30 minutes and by the time you end the practice, you will feel a lot lighter and relaxed. You will also feel a reliving relaxation of your spine.

To keep your root chakra spinning nicely, practice this exercise daily. By doing so, you start feeling more grounded, which helps stabilize the racing emotions and thoughts you often experience. You will also start focusing more on your survival, safety, and nourishment and will take better care of your needs related to these areas.

Sacral Chakra

Orange is the sacral chakra's color; this chakra, as stated earlier, relates to creativity, imagination, sexuality, and emotions. To cleanse your sacral chakra, imagine a bright orange colored light filling up the position of your sacral chakra. As the light grows brighter and bigger, it cleanses your sacral chakra off all sorts of blockages and negativities and the chakra spins faster.

To cleanse your sacral chakra of energy blockages, just as you visualized a red colored light filling your root chakra, visualize an orange colored glowing light entering and filling it completely.

As the light cleanses your sacral chakra, you shall start feeling emotionally better and your creative abilities shall start enhancing. As an empath, this helps you better understand and protect your emotions and use your innovative ability to discover how best to use your empathic abilities.

Solar plexus Chakra

The solar plexus chakra that governs your self-esteem and self-confidence associates with the color yellow. The color yellow associates with your will power, strength, and intellect; using it to cleanse your solar plexus chakra helps enhance your self-worth, self-esteem, and self-confidence.

To restore energy balance in your solar plexus chakra, visualize a beautiful, shiny yellow light filling in your upper abdomen: the location of your solar plexus chakra. Imagine the yellow light increasing in strength and magnitude and slowly eliminating all sorts of negativities from your solar plexus chakra.

By regularly practicing this visualization strategy, you slowly start to feel surer of yourself and your abilities. This helps you trust your special gift more and removes all sorts of uncertainties from your mind.

Many empaths who can sense spirits, invisible forces, and have the ability to feel the power and energy from inanimate objects, soil, and other beings feel unsure of their gift. They may also feel unhappy with their ability to feel everything to a heightened extent and want to get rid of their power because it overwhelms them.

If you have trouble managing emotions, cannot discern between which emotions are yours and which are not, and do not value yourself much, it is likely because you do not acknowledge and appreciate your gift. By cleansing your solar plexus chakra of energy blockages, you will overcome this issue and will become content and happy with your power.

Heart Chakra

Green is the color of the heart chakra; this color symbolizes love, compassion, integration, inner peace, and happiness. As an empath, one of your obligations is to spread happiness, love, and compassion everywhere. Doing so becomes nearly impossible when you do not feel happy with yourself and do not nurture self-love. This usually happens when there is an energy blockage in your heart chakra.

Cleansing your heart chakra helps energy flow smoothly through it, which ensures its spins properly. This helps you accept and acknowledge yourself and your gift, which paves way for self-love. Naturally, when you are pleased with yourself, you start feeling better about the things, and people around you, and can spread compassion, love, and happiness wherever you go.

To cleanse your heart chakra, sit comfortably in a quiet place just as you do while cleansing the other chakras; once you feel calm after taking a few cleansing breaths, imagine a green colored glow slowly filling up your heart center. With every deep breath you take, the green light grows bigger inside your heart chakra. Keep doing this for at least 15 minutes and in a little while, you will feel energized.

Regularly cleansing your heart chakra helps keep it open allowing energy to flow through it. This not only keeps you happy, it also helps your pink energy bubble grow bigger too.

Throat Chakra

Because they do not know how to express themselves properly, most empaths cannot succinctly communicate their concerns, needs, and feelings. This is mainly because of a blocked throat chakra. Your throat chakra regulates your self-expression and communication. When there is an energy blockage in this chakra, you are likely to experience problems in these areas.

As an empath, if you cannot communicate effectively or convey your viewpoint, feelings, and, nobody will focus on you. Instead, you will become the victim of constant demands; constant demands will overwhelm you and leave you feeling drained. If you face these issues, know that now is the time to purify your throat chakra to make it work efficiently.

To do that, with each deep breath you take, visualize a blue colored light entering your throat chakra and filling it completely. Continue doing this for 15 to 20 minutes and by the time you finish the practice, you feel stronger and more confident.

Since blue is the color of this chakra and the color associated with expression of truth, expression of your viewpoint, and communication with others, visualizing it regularly helps open and regulate your throat chakra.

Third Eye Chakra

Purifying your third eye chakra off negativities and energy blockages is imperative because unless you do so, you will not tap into your intuitive side, will not enhance your wisdom, and will not develop the ability to make sound decisions. Since your third eye chakra regulates all these areas, stabilizing it is important because when energy freely flows in this chakra, you gain the ability to make the best decisions for yourself as an empath and can better comprehend signals offered by your intuition.

To rinse out negativity from your third eye chakra, take the help of the indigo color since it is the color associated with your brow chakra. Indigo helps evoke your intuition and represents inner wisdom.

When you sit peacefully in a quiet room, take a few deep breaths, and slowly start envisioning a beautiful, indigo light slowly entering your third eye chakra and completely taking over it. Imagine the light's glow becoming shinier and bigger with every deep breath you take. Keep growing it until it clears out all sorts of unwanted elements and negativities from your brow chakra and makes it spin efficiently.

To keep your brow chakra clean and balanced, turn this practice into an everyday habit.

Crown Chakra

Empaths who have unleashed their full power are highly spiritual. In this case, being spiritual means these empaths have a clear sense of direction in life, know their needs and wants, and feel deeply connected to their spiritual side and the spiritual power they believe in.

To gain clarity of the path you want/ought to take in your life as an empath, it is crucially important that you tap into your spiritual side and unleash it. Doing so is easily possible by washing away impurities from your crown chakra and restoring energy balance in it.

To do that, visualize a violet colored light entering your crown chakra and then embracing it completely to the extent that the entire crown chakra starts glowing a violet light. As the light glows, the chakra starts to spin quickly and smoothly bringing harmony to your body and mind.

Violet is the color associated with connection with your spirituality, your consciousness, and your ability to connect with the power of the universe. Hence, visualizing it filling your crown chakra helps stabilize that chakra, thus helping you become more spiritual. As your spirituality improves, your ability to connect to the power of the universe and use its energy improves too. This consequently helps you protect yourself, your emotions, and your energy bubble.

Make sure you cleanse your chakras every day before going to bed so you wake up feeling fresh and active. As you get better at the practice, you will be able to do it faster. When you can easily cleanse all your chakras within minutes, habitually clean them a few times daily to keep them strong and harmonious.

While this helps enhance your energy, there is one more thing you need to do to keep yourself safe from undesirable energies and emotions: you need to meditate. Move to the next section to find out how meditation helps you and why you must do it.

USING THE POWER OF MEDITATION TO PROTECT YOUR ENERGY SHIELD

Adi Shankara, a philosopher and theologian from India said, *"As gold purified in a furnace loses its impurities and achieves its own true nature, through meditation, the mind gets rid of the impurities of the attributes of delusion, attachment, and purity, and attains Reality."*

Meditation purifies your heart, mind, and soul, and helps these three align so you attain complete purity, peace of mind, and harmony. Let us find out what meditation is and how it does this trick.

A Quick Insight into Meditation

Meditation is a simple tool that has the power to make you completely aware of your own self—your needs, emotions, thought process, thinking pattern, and behavior. When you have more and better self-awareness, you understand yourself better and know exactly what motivates and de-motivates you. In addition, you get better insight into your needs and do things that satisfy them. When you are an empath, being aware of yourself is gravely important to your ability to be happy and peaceful.

Meditation not only helps you cultivate and improve your sense of self-awareness, it also makes you more conscious of everyone and everything around you. Naturally, when you have better understanding of your surroundings and the people in it, you quickly become aware of an overwhelming situation and can immediately protect yourself from it so your energy does not come to any harm. By bringing your awareness to the present, meditation helps you achieve this goal.

Meditation Helps You Ground into Your Present

We often live in a state of forgetfulness; this forgetfulness comes from our worries of the past or future. As an empath, it is likely that you have had your fair share of this experience in more than one instance. Think of the time you were so worried about a friend that you completely disregarded your present wellbeing, or that one time when you could not forget a heart wrenching accident you saw on the road and because of this, for months on end, you could not get a good night's sleep. While these incidents do exhibit your compassionate side, they also show that you have the tendency to concentrate on your past. When you concentrate on the past, you are disregarding your present.

Not being aware of your present is exactly what makes you ignore your needs. When you dismiss your needs or are not conscious of them, you fail to take care of your energy and instead, you allow it to grow weak. To acknowledge your needs and to become more aware of them so you keep your energy protected from debilitating elements, it is paramount that you be mindful of yourself and your present. This is where meditation steps in to save the day.

Meditation improves your sense of awareness and helps you gradually focus more on the present moment without being judgmental of it. As you embrace the present, you start living in it, which helps you shun forgetfulness and become more aware and accepting of yourself.

By making meditation part of your life, you will stop worrying about others for days and will stop feeling overwhelmed. Instead of worrying about the past or future, you will start looking for presently available ways to help others and yourself. When you do this, you will end up helping others live a better life and will use your empathic abilities for overall good.

How to Practice Meditation

While there are many ways to practice meditation, here is a simple meditation practice ideal for beginner meditator/empaths. Here is how you can practice this technique to achieve these amazing results.

1. Sit in a calm, peaceful spot and breathe in your most natural way. Do not deepen or lengthen your breath.

2. Think of any happy memory and use it to calm yourself.

3. When you feel better, bring every ounce of your awareness to your breath and nothing but your breath. Focus on how you take an in-breath and how you exhale the air you inhaled.

4. As you concentrate on your breath, you may find your attention diverting to other 'irrelevant' thoughts. When that happens, tell yourself—in your head—that 'thinking has occurred' and bring your awareness back to your breath.

5. Start counting your breath from 1 to 10 and re-start at 1. Count one in-breath and one out-breath as 1 and continue doing so to the count of 10. This technique helps you focus on your breath.

6. When you start focusing better on your breath, think of there being a table right in front of where you are sitting.

7. Slowly divert your attention from your breath to all your worries and feelings and think of them. As different concerns start coming to your awareness, analyze each of them and put them on that table. Tune into your feelings just as you did when cleansing and protecting your energy and reflect on each emotion; this will help you figure out what belongs to you and what you picked from someone else.

8. Put your worries and emotions on one side of the table and those you absorbed from someone else on the other side. Take as much time as you need to do this practice. Once done, imagine shoving away all the foreign concerns, emotions, and feelings. Toss them off the table and imagine them evaporating into thin air; after they vanish, vow not to think of those issues again.

9. Do not move to your concerns placed on the table just yet. You will get a chance to deal with them later on.

10. Once you have dealt with the emotions and energies of others, take a few deep breaths to calm yourself. If you feel overwhelmed, try again the next day.

11. When you feel better, imagine you have no past or future because you were just born. You are basking in the blessings of a new life and you know you are an empath who God/the universe has given the opportunity to start afresh. Since you have just entered this world, you have no idea of what a past or future are and are only concerned about living in your present.

12. Take a few minutes or more to feel that way and when you can easily think of yourself having no past or future, focus on what needs, desires, or demands you have right now. Ask yourself questions such as *"What do I crave for?" "In which direction do I want to steer my life?" "What are my basic needs?" "How exactly do I feel about myself?" "How do I want to use my empathic abilities?" "How do I feel about being an empath?"* and other similar questions.

13. Deeply explore each question and its answer and write down these answers once you finish your meditation session. Doing this helps you become aware of your true needs and desires.

14. Once you deeply explore your new needs, return your awareness to your worries placed on the table, and start assessing them. If these worries, concerns, and needs are truly yours, you will feel the same way about them as you did earlier. However, if these were not your true needs, you

will care a lot less about them because you would have figured out your true needs and wishes.

15. Conduct a thorough comparison of the two until you understand how you feel about both: the concerns and needs you had previously, and your newfound wants and desires.

16. If any old need aligns with your new one and you feel connected to it, focus on it. However, if a certain need or concern you had previously seems meaningless, let it go.

By regularly practicing this meditation technique, you will soon gain better clarity of your needs, wants, and emotions and will start focusing on them.

Regularly write down all your needs, emotions, desires, and feelings and go through your journal entries daily so you can stay aware of how you feel as well as the improvement you experience in your feelings after you meditate. As you become better at meditation, you will start living in the present and will learn to understand and focus on your needs.

To protect your energy from energy leeches and vampires, you must also develop the ability to become quickly aware of any negativity around you the instant it manifests within your environment. This helps shield your energy. To ensure you keep your energy shield unbroken, strong, and beautiful, adopt a few of the strategies discussed in the next section.

ADDITIONAL EFFECTIVE ENERGY SHIELDING STRATEGIES

To make certain nobody infects your shield body, make the following practices part of your routine.

Set Boundaries for Everyone

As your sense of awareness improves, you will gain a better understanding of the people in your social circle and your environment. Find out which people in your social circle have a negative effect on your energy shield, those who weaken it.

Once you determine these people, gradually distance yourself from them. If for any reason, you cannot distance yourself from them, set well demarcated boundaries for them so they stop overwhelming and overpowering you. For instance, if your cousin is in the habit of making fun of how connected you feel to plants and animals, firmly tell him to keep his thoughts to himself and if that does not work, reduce your interaction with him.

Moreover, set limits for everyone in your life so they know when to, and when not to approach you with their problems, demands, and wishes. This keeps you safe from a constant barrage of worries and extra sentiments, allowing you to focus on yourself.

Additionally, set limits for yourself too. Find out which people, thoughts, situations, environments, and incidents upset you and get into the practice of distancing yourself from them. In addition, stop worrying about everyone else all the time to the point that it drains you. Whenever you find yourself doing that, tune into your feelings and cleanse your energy.

Convey Your Needs to Your Loved Ones

After setting boundaries for everyone including yourself, encourage yourself to go the extra mile and actually communicate your demands, needs, and wants to your family and loved ones. By now, you have enough awareness of what you want and how you want others to behave with you. It is time you start conveying your needs to them.

Inform your family of the sort of support you would like from them or how you would like them to cope with you when you feel frustrated. Moreover, clarify your sexual and survival needs and communicate these with your partner. For instance, if you are uncomfortable with one of your partner's sexual need, communicate your concern in as gentle a manner as possible, and tell your partner to fulfill his/her desires but you want his/her support and co-operation in exchange.

To feel good about yourself, you need to feel happy in every aspect of your life. When you feel good, your energy keeps growing too.

Take Warm/Cold Showers

Water does wonders for your shield body. It helps cleanse it of negativity, keeping it protected from all sorts of harms. Every day, take a warm or cold shower or bath depending on your needs. If you feel good taking a cold shower, enjoy it to feel grounded and restore energy balance to your body. If a warm bath is what does the trick for you, try that.

To cleanse your shield body of any unwanted element that may have stuck to it, get into the habit of taking a shower at least once daily. Moreover, showering daily improves your hygiene, which is another element that helps strengthen your shield body.

Use Incense and Essential Oils

We (humans) have used essential oils and incense for centuries to clear the environment of negative energies and to restore positivity. To ensure not even an ounce of negativity lingers in your environment or poisons your shield body, seek the help of essential oils and incense.

To clear the air around you of any negativity, burn cedar, sage, juniper, and sweet-grass incense. Alternatively, pour any essential oil you like in small jars and bottles and place them at different corners of your home. You can even massage your body with your favorite essential oil to protect your shield body against harmful emotions and energies.

To ensure your shield body stays safe and sound and helps your empathic abilities get better, try as many of these remedies as you can.

CONCLUSION

We have come to the end of the book. Thank you for reading and congratulations for reading until the end.

I hope you have found the book insightful.

Being an empath is special and amazing—not everyone has this beautiful power. However, the same power that gives you an edge over others can also sabotage you. To keep that from happening, follow the guidelines in the book to create a shield body that protects you for good and helps you unleash your full empath potential.

If you found the book valuable, can you recommend it to others? One way to do that is to post a review on Amazon.

Thank you and good luck!

Printed in Great Britain
by Amazon